TRANSPORTATION ADVENTURES

Written by
Doug Barone

IN THE AIR

KidHaven
PUBLISHING

Published in 2027 by
KidHaven Publishing, an Imprint of Greenhaven Publishing, LLC
2544 Clinton St., Buffalo, NY 14224

Written by: Doug Barone
Edited by: Rebecca Phillips-Bartlett
Designed by: Ker Ker Lee

Cataloging-in-Publication Data
Names: Barone, Doug.
Title: In the air / Doug Barone.
Description: Buffalo, NY : KidHaven Publishing, 2027. | Series: Transportation adventures | Includes glossary and index.
Identifiers: ISBN 9781534569744 (pbk.) | ISBN 9781534569751 (library bound) | ISBN 9781534569768 (ebook)
Subjects: LCSH: Flying-machines--Juvenile literature. | Aeronautics--History--Juvenile literature. | Transportation--History--Juvenile literature.
Classification: LCC TL547.B376 2027 | DDC 629.13--dc23

Printed in China

CPSIA compliance information: Batch #QS27KH: For further information contact Greenhaven Publishing LLC at 1-844-317-7404.

Photo Credits – Images courtesy of Shutterstock.com, unless otherwise stated.

Cover & Recurring – muratart, Soom02020. 2–3 – Synthetic Messiah. 4–5 – Monkey Business Images, Gorodenkoff. 6–7 – Rudmer Zwerver, Diagram Lajard, CC0 via Wikimedia Commons. 8–9 – Brian Reilly, Bogac Erkan. 10–11 – Stock for you, Romberi, Altrendo Images. 12–13 – frank_peters, Herget Josef. 14–15 – Sirbouman, aapsky, Herget Josef. 16–17 – Cobalt S-Elinoi, solocity. 18–19 – dnstudio, Carlos Calvo Torregrosa. 20–21 – Maridav, muratart. 22–23 – aapsky.

CONTENTS

Words that look like this can be found in the glossary on page 24.

TIME FOR AN ADVENTURE!

Transportation is the ways people get from place to place. Some forms of transportation offer you peaceful journeys. Others travel at high speeds. Many kinds can take you on an adventure!

IN THE AIR

For most of history, traveling through the air was just a dream. Today, people fly in the sky all the time. Have you ever flown before?

FLYING MACHINES

Inventors tried to come up with ways for humans to fly for hundreds of years. Many of these early ideas came from watching animals that fly, such as birds and bats.

Leonardo da Vinci was a famous painter and inventor in the 1400s and 1500s CE. He designed a number of flying machines. However, his designs were not really known about until 400 years after he died.

HOT-AIR BALLOONS

Hot-air balloons were the first vehicles that actually let people fly. Hot-air balloons have a basket for people to stand in. The first hot-air balloon flight was in France in 1783.

Hot-air balloons use a burner to heat up air. The hot air rises into the balloon. This rising air lifts the balloon up. This lifts the basket and the people inside off the ground.

AIRSHIPS

Airships, or blimps, use gases to fly. In the past, some airships used hydrogen. Today, airships are filled with helium. These gases are lighter than the air in the sky. This means they can float through the sky.

The first powered, steerable airship took off in 1852. It used a steam engine to move forward with a propeller. Since then, more powerful engines have been used to make airships faster.

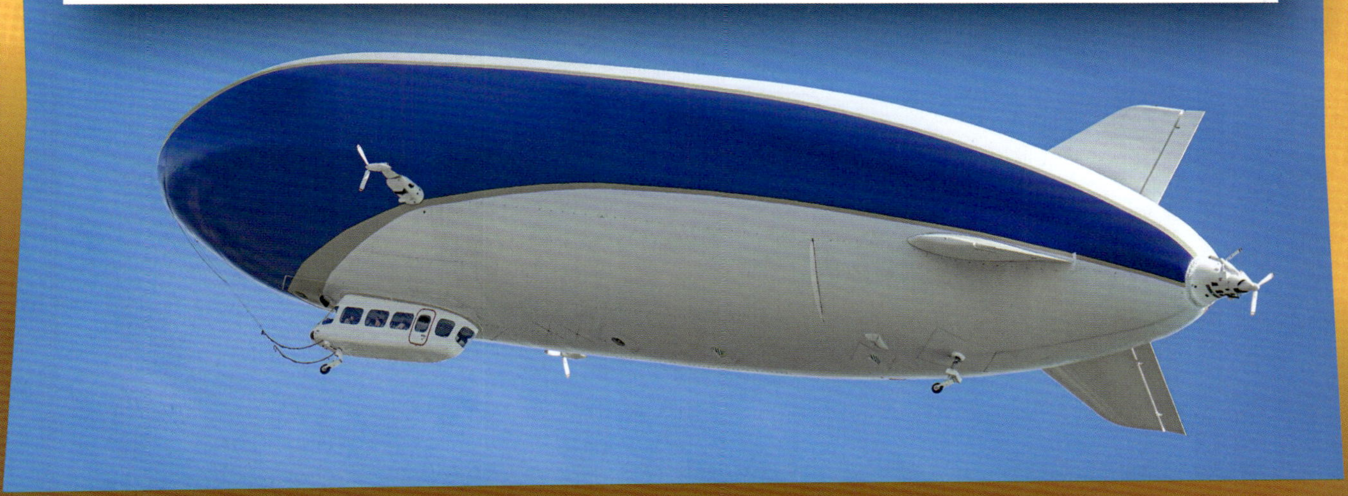

propeller

AIRPLANES

In 1903, the Wright brothers invented the first airplane successfully flown by a person. Its first flight lasted just 12 seconds. The Wright brothers inspired many other inventors.

Many of the earliest airplanes were biplanes. Biplanes have two wings stacked on top of each other. A combustion engine makes the propeller on the front of the plane spin. This creates thrust.

As engines became more powerful, monoplanes became more popular. Monoplanes have one main set of wings.

Today, most large airplanes use jet engines. Jet engines create a lot of power for larger and faster planes.

jet engine

One of the fastest passenger airplanes ever made was called the Concorde. It could fly at supersonic speeds. That means that it could go faster than the speed of sound!

HELICOPTERS

Inventors had experimented with vertical flight for years. Helicopters first became popular in the 1940s.

Helicopters have large blades on top and smaller blades on the tail. These blades spin, which makes helicopters fly.

Helicopter blades are curved on top and flat on the bottom. As they spin, air is pushed over the top faster than it is pushed underneath. This creates an upward force called lift.

JET PACKS

Have you ever wanted to freely fly across the sky? In recent years, inventors have been working on making jet packs. Jet packs are machines that a person wears to fly into the air.

Jet packs fly by burning fuel. When the fuel is burned, it creates a hot gas. The gas comes out of the jet pack toward the ground. This creates thrust, pushing the person in the jet pack up.

THE FUTURE OF TRANSPORTATION

Inventors are always hard at work coming up with new ways to fly in the air. If you were an inventor, what would you make?

Inventors have been trying to invent flying cars for a long time. Soon they could become a reality! Would you want to take a ride in a flying car?

TRANSPORTATION ADVENTURES

There are lots of different vehicles that can take people in the air. The science of flight has come a long way since Leonardo da Vinci's first drawings of flying machines.

These different modes of transportation can all be used to go on an adventure. Which vehicle would you like to fly in?

GLOSSARY

combustion	the act of burning or setting fire to something
force	a push or pull on an object
fuel	something that can be used to make energy or power something
gases	things that are like air, which fill any space available
steam engine	a machine that uses the gas made from heating water to power things
thrust	the force that makes an object move
vehicles	machines that are used to carry people or things
vertical	straight up and down

INDEX

BUG LIFE CYCLES

By Rod Barkman

EARTHWORM

KidHaven
PUBLISHING

Published in 2027 by
KidHaven Publishing, an Imprint of Greenhaven Publishing, LLC
2544 Clinton St., Buffalo, NY 14224

Written by: Rod Barkman
Edited by: Noah Leatherland
Designed by: Lucy Otter

Cataloging-in-Publication Data
Names: Barkman, Rod.
Title: Earthworm / Rod Barkman.
Description: Buffalo, NY : KidHaven Publishing, 2027. | Series: Bug life cycles | Includes glossary and index.
Identifiers: ISBN 9781534571150 (pbk.) | ISBN 9781534571167 (library bound) | ISBN 9781534571174 (ebook)
Subjects: LCSH: Earthworms--Juvenile literature. | Earthworms--Life cycles--Juvenile literature.
Classification: LCC QL391.A6 B37 2027 | DDC 592.64--dc23

Printed in China

CPSIA compliance information: Batch #QS27KH: For further information contact Greenhaven Publishing LLC at 1-844-317-7404.

Please visit our website, www.greenhavenpublishing.com.
For a free color catalog of all our high-quality books, call toll free 1-844-317-7404 or fax 1-844-317-7405.

Find us on

PHOTO CREDITS
All images are courtesy of Shutterstock.com, unless otherwise stated.

Cover – schankz. Recurring – Hemanthzoomn. 4–5 – Cristian Maciel06, oneinchpunch, Prostock-studio. 6–7 – domnitsky, VaskePro. 8–9 – Fevziie, Tomasz Klejdysz. 10–11 – Pong Wira, Vinicius Tupinamba. 12–13 – I Zoom, New Africa. 14–15 – Harusukae, Eka Jaya Permana. 16–17 – Majna, OMfotovideocontent. 18–19 – Craig Cordier, HumpPood, Lou Wagstaffe, CC BY-SA 4.0 < https://commons.wikimedia.org/wiki/File:Eisenia-hortensis-european-nightcrawler.jpg> via Wikimedia Commons. 20–21 – Bukhta Yurii, nexusby. 22–23 – Art_Pictures, jutamatk, Natasha Wood, Tomasz Klejdysz.